THELWELL'S BOOK OF LEISURE

Also by Norman Thelwell

ANGELS ON HORSEBACK
THELWELL COUNTRY
THELWELL IN ORBIT
A PLACE OF YOUR OWN
A LEG AT EACH CORNER
TOP DOG
THELWELL'S RIDING ACADEMY
UP THE GARDEN PATH
THELWELL'S COMPLEAT TANGLER

First published in 1968 by Methuen & Co Ltd
and printed in Great Britain
by Ebenezer Baylis and Son, Ltd
The Trinity Press, Worcester, and London
Reprinted 1968
SBN 416 12010 5
1·2

:thelwell's.
BOOK of LEISURE

METHUEN & CO LTD

The enjoyment of life—

"Don't you *ever* relax, J.B.?"

—is an attitude of mind

"She wants to know if she can have another hour?"

Some like to take their leisure in the open air

"Oh for pity's sake let him light it."

Others prefer to relax quietly at home

But whether one is rich—

"Money can't buy them happiness."

—or poor

"Charlie and I are staying at Dingle Halt to-morrow night, then on to Amberley Tracy, Cherry Candover, Wilton in Arden and down to the coast."

There's an interest somewhere for everyone.

Leisure on wheels

"It's rejected the new carburettor."

"There are three slugs and a woodlouse in the glove boot."

"I've got a three-litre Rover at the moment – about a mile outside Salford."

"We were lucky in more ways than one, I suppose."

"Oh for heaven's sake – take him through again."

"That looks a nice spot."

"Fiat 500, E Type Jag, Hillman Husky, Austin Mini-Cooper S., Daimler S.P. 250 . . . "

"Give us a shout if things are starting to move, mate!"

"You've smashed my best china."

"Your dinner's in the oven."

"We've got a broken spring – in the nearside mattress."

"Aren't you out of bed yet?"

"We can never catch the visitors at it, m'lord."

Messing about....

"I should have known when I saw the self-steering gear."

"I'm sorry, mate, it's a single-handed race."

"Attention all shipping!"

"I didn't spot that pollution 'til it was too late."

"It gets them really white and it's kind to my hands."

"It makes me livid. Five thousand nine hundred quid and then you get sneered at."

"You should spot the pier any moment. We're going through the sewage now."

"And even if we do get back, I bet all the moorings are taken."

31

"Did you see what he called you?"

"I remember one terrible night back in sixty-three, on the Chiswick Flyover."

"Hullo! It's started."

Strictly for the birds . . .

"If we're very quiet we might see Peter Scott."

"Steady on Charlie! It's on the Protected List."

"We must have dozed off."

"It says here – 'Please return to the Wildfowl Trust'."

"I fed it and cared for it until its wing was better again – but when I came to release it . . ."

"It's not oil. They've been gassed."

The BIRD LOVER'S BOOK

Relaxing at home

"What date do we open to the public?"

"This'll shake the Duke of Bedford! We picked up fifty-six tons more litter than he did last season."

"You can't help but like them – they don't care a damn."

"This always has to happen when we've got company."

"Careful! Those little sticks are sharp."

"Is there anyone you don't know?"

"You're not circulating, Mr. Wilkins."

"What! *This* dreadful old thing?"

Away from it all

"Don't get flustered."

"I've got all the postcards written anyway."

"Let it down or carry it yourself."

"What on earth do you want your knitting for?"

"Oh, by the way, she's expecting pups any day."

"I told you to cancel it."

"This could save the match for England."

"Don't make it sound *too* good. They're mowing our lawns whilst we're away, remember."

"Isn't that our au pair girl?"

The inner man . . .

"What! Frozen fish fingers for lunch again?"

"My compliments to the Chef."

"Thank God! It's the lemons!"

"A Merry Christmas, Humphries."

"Ho-ho! Who's been watering the damn' beer then?"

"These damn' chemical sprays are ruining all our food – even the hedgehogs."

"*Please*, Sid! Just a drop to get the fire going?"

Leisurely pastimes

"Don't worry, darling. You can have some new jodhpurs for Christmas."

"Hat off in the house."

"Sandra's pony's broken a leg."

"He knocked down the last fence – with my foot."

"There goes his Duke of Edinburgh Award."

"You never hear anything about testing *their* breath."

"May heaven forgive you."

"He got sent off on purpose."

"Come on, England!"

"I suppose to you, that's perfection."